THE FRUITS OF THE SPIRIT

WRITTEN BY

MISHTY MEISHERI

ILLUSTRATIONS BY

AMELIA SINTA

notionpress.com

INDIA · SINGAPORE · MALAYSIA

ISBN 979-8-89744-653-7

THIS BOOK BELONGS TO

THIS BOOK IS DEDICATED TO

ABIGAIL & DINAH

(SISTERS IN CHRIST)

Ðear Children,
God gives us fruits to help us grow,
To love like Jesus and to show,
That the Holy Spirit makes us strong,
Guiding our hearts all day long.
The Bible tells us, clear and true,
These special fruits shine bright in you.

"But the fruit of the Spirit is love, joy, peace, forbearance, kindness, goodness, faithfulness, gentleness and self-control."

- Galatians 5:22-23

Each fruit helps us to share
God's love,
A special gift from up above.

We'll learn them all, one by
one,
And spread His Word to
everyone...

LOVE

LOVE

Love means caring for others
each day,
Giving hugs and kind words
along the way.

"We love because He first loved us."
- John 4:19

JOY

JOY

Joy is a happy, a heart full of light,
Smiling and laughing because everything is alright.

"the joy of the Lord is your strength."
- Nehemiah 8:10

PEACE

PEACE

Peace is staying calm, even
when you are mad,
Using soft words, instead of
being bad.

"Peace I leave with you; my peace I give you."
- John 14:27

PATIENCE

PATIENCE

Patience is waiting with a
happy heart,
Not crying or whining when
things fall apart.

"Be completely humble and gentle; be patient,
bearing with one another in love."
- Ephesians 4:2

KINDNESS

KINDNESS

Kindness is sharing and
helping a friend,
Being nice to others again and
again.

"Be kind and compassionate to one another, forgiving each other, just as in Christ God forgave you."
- Ephesians 4:32

GOODNESS

GOODNESS

Goodness is choosing to do
what is right,
Even when no one is in sight.

"Do not be overcome by evil, but overcome evil with
good."
- Romans 12:21

FAITHFULNESS

FAITHFULNESS

Faithfulness means trusting
every day,
Loving God and always
obeying His way.

"Great is Your faithfulness."
- Lamentations 3:23

GENtLENESS

GENTLENESS

Gentleness is using soft hands
and words,

Speaking sweetly so no hearts
would be hurt.

"Let your gentleness be evident to all. the Lord is
near."
- Philippians 4:5

SELF-CONTROL

SELF-CONTROL

Self-control is stopping when
we should,
Saying "NO" to wrong and
choosing good.

"For the Spirit God gave us does not make us timid,
but gives us power, love and self-discipline."
- 2 Timothy 1:7

LOVE
JOY
PEACE
PATIENCE
KINDNESS
GOODNESS
FAITHFULNESS
GENTLENESS
SELF-CONTROL

God gives us fruits to help us grow,
In love and kindness, this we know.

When we listen and obey,
Joy and peace will fill our day.

Let's share these gifts in all we do,
So God's great love shines bright in you!